PIANO FOR ADULTS

LEVEL FOUR

by WESLEY SCHAUM

Teacher Consultants: Alfred Cahn, Joan Cupp, Sue Pennington

INDEX

SCHAUM PUBLICATIONS, INC.

10235 N. Port Washington Rd.   Mequon, WI 53092
© Copyright 1994 by Schaum Publications, Inc., Mequon, Wisconsin
International Copyright Secured   All Rights Reserved
Printed in U.S.A.

 *printed on recycled paper*

01-54
HG-2

FOREWORD

This method is tailored for an older individual — adult or teen-ager. It may also be used for mature students of a younger age.

The progress here is much more gradual than other adult methods. This allows the student to be entirely comfortable with the learning steps. The rate of progress is flexible; work in this book can be leisurely or fast paced, depending upon the individual pupil and preference of the teacher.

The musical excerpts are themes from symphonies, operas, ballets, concertos, oratorios, chamber music, vocal and choral literature. Also included are folk songs from many ethnic groups. No simplified *piano* music is used. Music appreciation stories of the musical and biographical information and portraits of the composers are provided.

Systematic review of the various learning elements is provided by a planned variety of key signatures, time signatures, tempos and musical styles. This enhances the educational appeal and provides a series of modest challenges to the student.

A reference page, correlating notes and keyboard position along with basic musical symbols, is found on the front inside cover and continued on the back inside cover. A music dictionary, appropriate for level four, is provided on pages 46-47. The index on page 48 helps to locate explanations contained within the method.

MUSICIANSHIP CURRICULUM

Sound musicianship is attained by thorough musical study, and staying on each level until it is mastered. It is intended that this method book be part of a systematic approach to learning to play the piano. This is done by working in four books at the same level before moving up to the next level.

1. Method 2. Theory 3. Technic 4. Repertoire

This 4-book curriculum may be tailored to each individual student, depending on age, ability and interests. Here are the Schaum supplements available at this level. At least one book should be assigned in each category, with preference to the first title in each group:

THEORY Books: THEORY WORKBOOK, Level 4
                        INTERVAL SPELLER

TECHNIC Books: FINGERPOWER, Level 4

REPERTOIRE Books: CLASSICS of RENOWN, Bk 1   CHRISTMAS SOLOS, Level 4
                         BEST of BACH   HYMNS and GOSPEL SONGS
                         BEST of BEETHOVEN   NUTCRACKER SUITE
                         BEST of MOZART   RHYTHM and BLUES, Bk 3

SHEET MUSIC May Also Be Used For REPERTOIRE - see page 47.

Optional Book Featuring CHORD SYMBOLS and IMPROVISING:
EASY KEYBOARD HARMONY, Book 3

(All Books are Published by Schaum Publications, Inc.)
For additional suggestions of supplementary books and sheet music solos, ask for a free copy of the "Schaum Teachers Guide."

CONTENTS

Memorizing Hints

Careful daily practice, while learning a piece, lays the foundation for memorizing. Unfortunately, mistakes are easily memorized. Therefore, practicing the *correct* notes and rhythm, using proper fingering, and observing dynamics, phrasing and pedal marks are all necessary in order to memorize accurately.

As with choices for repertoire, select pieces that you feel comfortable playing. A favorite short piece is a good starting place to gain experience. Begin by memorizing a piece one or two phrases at a time; this can be spread out over several days or weeks. Do not worry about the rest of the piece yet. If necessary, memorize one hand at a time. Start with the right hand alone, next do the left hand alone, then combine both hands. Humming the melody notes as you play is another effective way to help your memory. Even though it may be tempting to play the entire piece, concentrate only on the part you are memorizing that day.

Memorizing involves several steps. The first is a process of awareness and analysis. *Become aware* of the musical form and patterns in the melody and accompaniment. *Become aware* of the physical movements that combine to produce a performance. Next, *organize* the music in your mind, then gradually establish the music in memory through careful and systematic practice.

Performing a piece of music is a mental and a physical process that involves the coordination of several senses.

Sense of Touch. Be aware of the *feeling* in your fingers and hands as you play various intervals and chords, as you make thumb and finger crossings, and as you change hand position. Recognize the *feeling* in your fingers and hands as you play **pp**, **mp**, **f**, etc. The feeling in your foot as you make the pedal movements is also important.

Sense of Hearing. Listen for the *sounds* of the melody and accompaniment. These sounds can be grouped into phrases and accompaniment patterns. Be aware of the *sounds* of various harmonies, dynamics, accents, tempo changes, pedal changes, etc.

Sense of Sight. Watch for the *look* of the page of music, especially the form and various phrases. Recognize the *look* of places in the music where there are hand position changes, wide intervals and chords. Be aware of the *contour* of various melody and accompaniment patterns. Watch for the *location* of various dynamic marks, pedal marks, repeat signs, 1st and 2nd endings, etc.

Organizing. The musical form of a composition is important in organizing your memory work. Recognizing musical patterns in the melody and accompaniment also makes memorizing easier. Look for the repetitions of these patterns. Phrase marks in the *treble* staff will help locate melody patterns. Phrase marks in the *bass* staff often indicate accompaniment patterns, many of which are broken chords. If helpful, use a pencil to indicate the sections of musical form and repeated patterns. Broken chord patterns may be indicated by chord symbols.

The organizing needed for memorization can be done by establishing mental "signposts" or "markers" along the way, perhaps every four measures. This is similar to navigating a ship by using buoys, lighthouses and other landmarks as guides. The markers may be elements of the musical form, patterns in the melody and accompaniment, changes of dynamics, repeat signs, changes of hand position, particular chords or harmonies, or pedal patterns. The choice of such markers is a personal one. Use whatever works for you. The markers may differ from one piece to another.

It may be helpful to make a cassette tape recording of the piece, using the music, and then listening to the tape to help determine which markers would be helpful to you during memorizing. Also use a cassette tape to evaluate your memorized playing.

Make a "cue card" for each memorized piece, listing the musical form and other markers you have chosen. This may help to organize your memory. Make note of the slight differences in the form such as **A** and **A**^{1}. Likewise, make note of similar phrases with slight differences in notes, rhythms or harmonies.

Memorizing requires concentration and mental discipline that focuses your attention on the processes which contribute to your playing of the music. Don't let your mind wander. During practice, try to minimize any distractions or noises that may interfere with your concentration. As you gain confidence and develop the **habit of focusing your attention**, you will become less disturbed by distractions.

This description of the memorizing process sounds more complicated than it is. Many of the elements involving the sense of touch, hearing and sight are well developed during practicing when you begin learning a piece. Memorizing involves going one step beyond because it organizes and coordinates the elements of playing a piece, and carefully focuses your attention as you do additional practicing.

As an incentive, you should plan various occasions to share your memorized pieces with others. This may be simply for a close friend or a small family group.

Successful Practice Ideas

The time you spend will be much more productive if you can **focus your full attention on practicing** and minimize interruptions. The *quality of practice* is more important than the amount of time you spend. This means organizing your practicing. A lesson assignment book or notebook is very helpful for this purpose. Your teacher will help you set your practice objectives each week.

Learn to recognize the difference between practicing and playing. Practice should always have a definite goal. When first learning a piece, your purpose may simply be to play the correct notes at a very slow tempo. As you continue to practice, you should try to gradually increase the speed until the performance tempo is achieved. Problems with fingering, rhythm, dynamics, phrasing or pedaling should be systematically improved. Usually, it is better to concentrate on one thing at a time rather than attempting too much at once.

Regular practicing is essential to success. It is much better to have five or six short practice sessions spread out during the week, than spending two hours practicing the night before your lesson. Piano playing requires a surprising amount of muscular control and coordination. Although this involves mainly small movements of the arms and fingers, the physical skills are nonetheless similar to playing tennis or golf. These should be developed gradually during practice.

Try not to let more than one day go by without some practicing, even if you spend only ten or fifteen minutes. Shorter practice periods are easier to fit into a busy schedule.

There is also value in playing just for fun. Playing favorite pieces that are not on your practice list is good review, helps maintain finger dexterity and adds confidence to your playing. It is also worthwhile to explore new music. You should consult with your teacher, however, before going ahead in any of your music books.

Precise Rhythm: Dotted 8th +16th note vs. Two 8th notes

This piece contains many measures with a dotted 8th +16th note rhythm and also a two 8th note rhythm, as in the first two measures. Be very careful to *differentiate* between the two rhythmic patterns. This requires that you **watch the notes carefully,** count carefully and listen for the correct rhythm.

Hail To The Chief (Sanderson)

DIRECTIONS: There are many changes of hand position in this piece. Be sure to follow the fingering carefully. Learn to play the notes with the correct rhythm first, then add the pedal.

THE PRESIDENT'S MARCH − This march is played to recognize and introduce the President of the United States at official visits and ceremonies. It was first used about 1828 and has become the President's "theme song." It is said to have been a favorite of Woodrow Wilson, who was president between 1913 and 1921. The title, "Hail To The Chief," comes from part of the epic poem, "Lady of the Lake," by Sir Walter Scott.

James Sanderson (1769-1841) was an English theater conductor, composer, violinist and teacher in London. He wrote the music for numerous plays, pantomimes, musical shows and light operas.

6

D.S. al fine – Introduction

D.S. is an abbreviation of **dal segno** (dahl SEN-yoh) meaning *the sign* (𝄋). **D.S. al fine** means to return to the sign and play to the measure marked **fine**.

In this piece, the first ten measures are an *introduction*. The introduction is separated from the main melody by a double bar. The *sign* (for the D.S.) is located in measure 11, where the main melody begins.

On the Beautiful Blue Danube, Op. 314 (Strauss, 1867) – see page 11

DIRECTIONS: The treble clef part contains both melody and accompaniment notes. The accompaniment notes have been marked **pp**. The damper pedal is held down for almost three measures, while these soft treble accompaniment notes are played.

JOHANN STRAUSS, JR. – See the bottom of page 11 for information on this composer and the music.

To be used with this method book: **THEORY WORKBOOK, Level 4** – Includes Recognition of Major and Minor Triads, Syncopated Rhythms, Transposing by Interval, 1st and 2nd Inversions of Triads, 6th Chords and 7th Chords.

8

Rallentando (abbreviated rall.)
Rallentando (rah-lenn-TAHN-doh) means *gradually growing slower.* It means the same as **rit.** (ritardando).

Accidental in Parenthesis
An accidental in parenthesis is a *reminder* to cancel the accidental from the previous measure. Because a bar line cancels all previous accidentals, the accidental is not really necessary, thus parenthesis are used.

Londonderry Air (Irish Folk Song)
DIRECTIONS: This piece is in the key of E-flat major; be sure to observe the three flats in the key signature.
The pedal is irregular; be careful to make the pedal changes accurately. Notice that **rall.** is used *twice* in the last line of music.

VALUE of REVIEW – Reviewing is an opportunity to enjoy what you have already learned, to add refinements to the music and gain confidence in your playing. It is a good idea to review 2 or 3 pieces regularly by playing them several times each week. Unless your teacher has a specific purpose in asking you to review, you may pick out any favorite pieces previously learned. It is a good experience to go back to one of your previous books or sheet music and play through some of that music.

Melody Alternating Between Hands

The first 8 measures have the melody in the *left* hand, the next 8 measures have the melody in the *right* hand. This alternating pattern continues for the remainder of the piece. As a reminder, **basso marcato** is printed where the left hand melody sections begin; **melodia marcato** is printed where the right hand melody section begins.

The musical form, **A - A¹ - B - A¹,** is indicated by red letters at the beginning of each section. Notice that the form coincides with each change of melody from one hand to the other. The **A¹** section has the melody in the right hand instead of the left hand. The final **A¹** of the form is the D.S. section.

German Dance No. 1 (Beethoven, 1795) – see page 11

DIRECTIONS: The printed dynamic marks are for the melody. The accompaniment should always be softer. *Listen carefully* to be sure that the *accompaniment is always played softly.* The melody should be heard clearly at all times regardless of the dynamic mark. Be sure there is no delay when going back to the D.S. section. This piece has no pedal due to the quickly moving 8th notes.

10

9/8 Time Signature

All of the note and rest values in 9/8 time are the same as in 6/8 time. Counting numbers have been printed in red for several measures. Notice the use of the **dotted quarter rest.** In 9/8 time it gets 3 counts, the same as a dotted quarter note.

Serenade ("Ständchen") D-920 (Schubert, 1827) – see page 11

DIRECTIONS: As a preparatory, count and tap the treble clef rhythm with the right hand and simultaneously tap the bass clef rhythm with the left hand. If necessary, count and tap the rhythm for each clef separately.

At first, learn to play the notes without pedal. Add pedal after the notes and rhythm can be played with confidence.

If desired, the D minor scale on page 18 may be learned as a supplemental exercise.

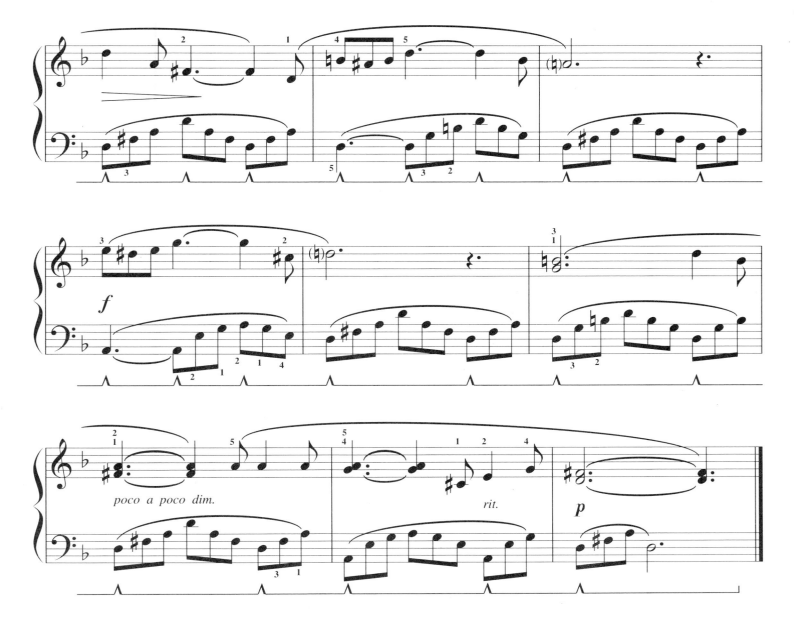

Page 6: JOHANN STRAUSS, JR. (also known as Johann Strauss II) 1825-1899 – Austria
The famous "waltz king" was an enormously popular composer and conductor in Vienna. At the time, it was customary to conduct a dance orchestra while holding a violin and playing along during the most important passages. Oddly, Strauss' father, who was also a successful Viennese dance orchestra leader and composer, forbade him to study the violin and wanted him to go into a business career instead. However, with his mother's help, Strauss secretly studied the violin and went on to become a renowned musician.

The "Blue Danube" is Strauss' most famous waltz and its main theme is probably one of the best known melodies ever written. It was composed for orchestra and performed both for concerts and for ballroom dancing. The original version is quite lengthy and consists of five waltzes, each with two themes. This arrangement uses the two themes from the first waltz section.

Page 9: LUDWIG VAN BEETHOVEN (BAY-toe-ven) 1770-1827 – Germany
In 1792 Beethoven moved to Vienna, Austria, where he remained for the rest of his life. There he studied with Haydn and with Salieri (Mozart's rival). Beethoven made his first public appearance in Vienna in 1795, playing the solo for one of his piano concertos. During the same year he wrote a set of 12 short dances for small orchestra. The "German Dance" is the first in this set. Although it is folk-like in style, it is not a folk tune.

He became very popular as a concert pianist and composer and was frequently an invited guest at aristocratic social gatherings in Vienna. Incidentally, Beethoven was fond of dancing although he was not a good dancer!

Page 10: FRANZ SCHUBERT (SHOO-burt) 1797-1828 – Austria
Schubert composed hundreds of songs written for various solo voices and vocal combinations, most with piano accompaniment. The "Serenade" was composed at the request of a friend who wanted a new song as a surprise birthday present to her pupils. Schubert originally wrote it as an alto (female voice) solo with a 3-voice male choral accompaniment and piano. When he found out that the pupils were all girls, he wrote a second version with a female chorus. Although he did not attend the birthday party, when Schubert first heard it performed, he remarked about the beauty of the music and was apparently very pleased. Much later, it was one of his personal choices played at a private concert of his own music, just a few months before his death.

Review: Key of E Major
There are four sharps in the key signature for E Major. They are (from left to right) F#, C#, G# and D#. This *sequence of sharps is always the same.* The 1st sharp (farthest to left) is always F#; the 2nd is always C#; the 3rd is always G#; the 4th is always D#.

Carnival of Venice (Italian Folk Song)

DIRECTIONS: Folk music, because of its origins, often has versions that differ, sometimes just slightly. If this melody is familiar, there may be notes or rhythms printed here which are different than what you remember. Be sure to *play the notes as written,* not as you remember them. The pedal movement is irregular; be sure to observe the markings carefully.

Frequent Changes of Time Signature

This piece has many changes of time signature; however, they all follow a pattern and the beat does not change. Two measures of "common" time (4/4) are followed by one measure of 2/4 time. This pattern occurs four times, once in each line of music.

It is very important that you MAINTAIN A STEADY BEAT throughout all the changes of time signature.

Natural Accents

When playing music, you may be aware of a small pulse on the first count of every measure. It is more of an internal feeling than an actual accent. It helps you to maintain a steady beat and organize the rhythm in your mind. This is called a **natural accent.**

A change of time signature causes a *shift* of the natural accent. This may be uncomfortable at first and will require some concentration to get the feeling for the rhythm.

Chippewa Moccasin Game (Native American)

DIRECTIONS: When one repeat sign is used alone at the end, it means to go back to the beginning and play the entire piece again. If desired, the E minor scale on page 19 may be learned as a supplemental exercise.

NATIVE AMERICAN MUSIC — Like most folk music, native American music evolved as it was passed on by memory from one generation to another. This melody is an authentic Chippewa tribal theme collected by Charles G. Willson. The moccasin game was played with a black bead. The object was to find the person whose moccasin covered the bead.

Three–Staff Reading

Three staffs are sometimes used for a cross-hand accompaniment, as in this piece. At the beginning, each staff is labeled L.H. or R.H. Notice that the left hand is to play the notes on the bottom staff and then cross over to also play the top staff notes. The bottom two staffs each have a bass clef. All three staffs are joined by a brace at the beginning of each line.

Were You There? (African–American Spiritual)

DIRECTIONS: The melody notes should always be heard clearly and the accompaniment subdued. Watch for separate dynamic marks for the melody and for the cross-hand accompaniment.

Be careful to **maintain a steady beat as you play the cross-hand accompaniment**. To accomplish this, you may need to practice very slowly at first while getting accustomed to crossing back and forth in the left hand. The cross over must be done without any slowing or delay of the beat.

The damper pedal is especially important in cross hand playing because it helps to smooth over the wide leaps in the accompaniment. Be sure to play the pedal part accurately.

On the 4th beat of measure 8, the right hand melody note *fits between* the two notes of the left hand. In measures 9 through 12 the left hand does not cross over. The **hold** in measure 15 should be held the equivalent of 2 or 3 beats.

To be used with this method book: **FINGERPOWER, Level 4** – Progressive Technic Exercises that *help develop finger strength*. Includes Trills in Thirds, Tremolo, Grace Notes, Thumb Passages, Finger Expansion, Two Octave Arpeggios, Scales in Contrary Motion, Legato Triads and Thirds, Arpeggios in Triplets and Chromatic Hand Contractions.

USING A METRONOME — The metronome numbers used in this book indicate a range of recommended tempo, the slowest to the fastest. You may, of course, use any tempo between the two numbers shown. <u>Be sure to observe the note value used with the numbers</u>. Although it is often a quarter note, other notes may be used.

In some music the letters **M.M.** (Maelzel's Metronome) appear with the numbers; these letters make no difference in the use or setting of the metronome. Unless you are playing in a contest or audition, the metronome speed is advisory and not mandatory. Often there is just one number to indicate the speed; consult with your teacher if you think a different tempo is more suitable.

A metronome may be helpful when new rhythms are encountered or if there is difficulty in maintaining a steady beat. When practicing, it is advisable to use a *much slower speed to start* and gradually increase the tempo as you gain proficiency.

You should not become dependent upon the metronome by using it too much. Your teacher can advise you on its proper use. Use the metronome for a few measures to get a feeling for the tempo you want and then practice without it. Excessive use of the metronome will seriously interfere with the proper performance of **rall.**, **rit.**, **accel.**, and the **fermata** (hold).

Multi-Word Tempo Marks

Many pieces have tempo marks with two or more words. There is usually one word which indicates the speed and others which make modifications. In this piece, **allegro** is the word which indicates the speed, **moderato** is the modifier. When combined they mean "moderately fast."

Dissonance

This piece has several places where the melody and accompaniment notes seem to clash. These dissonances are intentional; this is the reason for the natural sign in measure 2. The natural sign is in parentheses as a reminder, since an accidental applies only to the note at one pitch and in one staff.

Dark Eyes (Russian Gypsy Folk Song)

DIRECTIONS: This piece uses a 3/8 time signature. The note values are the same as for 6/8 time. Counting numbers are printed in red at the beginning. At the beginning, two 8th rests are used in the bass clef. It would also be correct to substitute one quarter rest, but the 8th rests are preferred because the 8th note gets one count. Although a **rit.** is often found at the end of a piece, it may also occur in other places as here in the 3rd line.

This piece has many unusual harmonies, especially in the last six measures. Watch to be sure you are playing the correct notes. A new low bass note, B, is found in the last full measure.

If desired, the B minor scale on page 19 may be learned as a supplemental exercise.

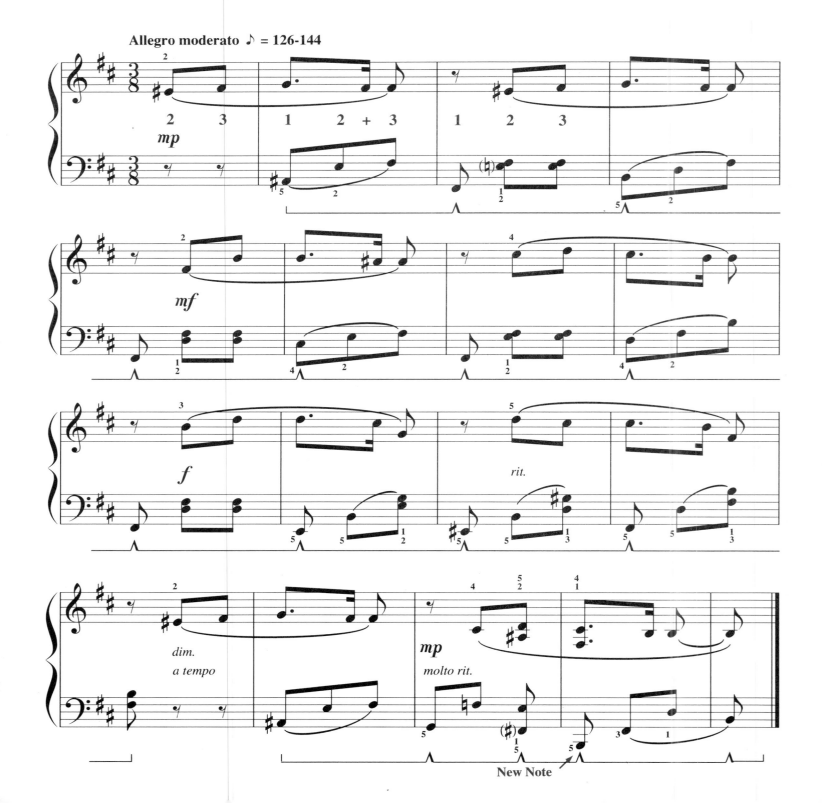

Phrasing As a Clue to Hand Position

The left hand accompaniment has many changes of hand position involving wide intervals. The bass clef slurs (short phrases) show the notes which are to be played in one hand position, and help to visualize the necessary hand movements.

Black Is the Color of My True Love's Hair (American Folk Song)*

DIRECTIONS: As a preparatory, play the left hand alone without pedal; then play the left hand alone with pedal.

This piece is in the key of C minor; it is related to the key of E-flat major because it has the same key signature.

The instruction **8va**, below the final note, means to play that note *one octave lower.*

*This version is based on an arrangement by John W. Schaum.

Harmonic Minor Scale Construction

The most commonly used minor scale is the **harmonic** minor. It consists of eight notes in musical alphabet order; each note has a number name called a **degree**. The harmonic minor scale has a special sequence of half steps and whole steps and includes a unique wide interval of 1½ steps.

The staff below shows the A harmonic minor scale with degree numbers printed in red. The letters between the notes indicate the step size.   H = Half Step   W = Whole Step   1½ = 1½ Step

Relative Major

Every minor scale has a relative major scale. They are related because they have the **same key signature.**

A Minor Scale (Harmonic Minor) – *The Relative Major is C Major*

DIRECTIONS: Practice each scale, hands separately, several times per day until it can be played easily and accurately. Scale degree numbers are printed in red. Finger numbers are printed in black. Be careful to keep playing legato at places where the *thumb goes under* and where fingers *cross over* the thumb. Try to avoid excessive motion of the wrist and forearm when the thumb is crossed under.

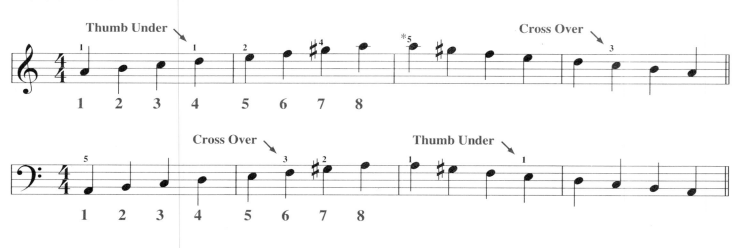

D Minor Scale (Harmonic Minor) – *The Relative Major is F Major*

DIRECTIONS: Practice each scale, hands separately, several times per day until it can be played easily and accurately. Scale degree numbers are printed in red. Finger numbers are printed in black. Be careful to keep playing legato at places where the *thumb goes under* and where fingers *cross over* the thumb.

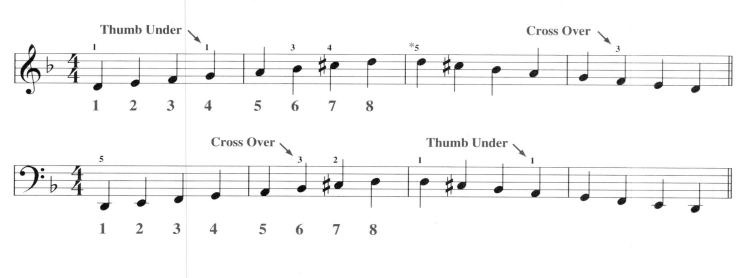

Teacher's Note: The scales on pages 18 and 19 need NOT be learned at the same time. They may be done individually, according to your preference, along with pieces in the same key. A scale may be used as a warm-up for a piece which is in the same key as the scale.

* The fingering will have to be adjusted when two or more octaves are played.

E Minor Scale (Harmonic Minor) – *The Relative Major Is G Major*

DIRECTIONS: Practice each scale, hands separately, several times per day until it can be played easily and accurately. Scale degree numbers are printed in red. Finger numbers are printed in black. Be careful to keep playing legato at places where the *thumb goes under* and where fingers *cross over* the thumb.

B Minor Scale (Harmonic Minor) – *The Relative Major is D Major*

DIRECTIONS: Practice each scale, hands separately, several times per day until it can be played easily and accurately. Scale degree numbers are printed in red. Finger numbers are printed in black. Be careful to keep playing legato at places where the *thumb goes under* and where fingers *cross over* the thumb.

G Minor Scale (Harmonic Minor) – *The Relative Major is B-flat Major*

DIRECTIONS: Practice each scale, hands separately, several times per day until it can be played easily and accurately. Scale degree numbers are printed in red. Finger numbers are printed in black. Be careful to keep playing legato at places where the *thumb goes under* and where fingers *cross over* the thumb.

* The fingering will have to be adjusted when two or more octaves are played.

For a more detailed presentation of major and harmonic minor scales, use the **Schaum SCALE SPELLER**.

Review: Grace Notes

The grace notes in this piece should be played *slightly ahead* of the 4th beat, so that the principal note is played precisely on the 4th beat.

Review: Harmonic Minor

A descending harmonic minor scale is found in the melody in measures 7 and 8.

Funeral March of a Marionette (Gounod, 1872)

DIRECTIONS: Counting numbers are printed in red at the beginning. In measure 2, treble clef, notice the 8th rest between the two notes beamed together on the 1st and 3rd beats. This form of notation is used in several places in this piece and is found often in other music using a 3/8, 6/8, or 9/8 time signature.

If desired, the G minor scale on page 20 may be learned as a supplemental exercise.

CHARLES GOUNOD (GOO-noh) 1818 -1893 – France

Among musicians, Gounod is remembered for the opera "Faust," and over 200 songs, which are considered his best music. He also wrote 11 other operas and numerous pieces of sacred music.

His best known melody is probably "Ave Maria" which uses a Bach "Prelude in C Major" as the accompaniment. The familiar "Funeral March of a Marionette" was written for orchestra, and 100 years later achieved fame as the theme of the TV mystery series "The Alfred Hitchcock Hour."

D.C. al Coda

D.C. is the abbreviation of **da capo** (dah KAH-poh) meaning to return to the beginning.

A **coda** (KOH-dah) is a musical section at the ending of a piece.

   D.C. al coda means to return to the beginning and play to the first coda sign (⊕); then skip to the second coda sign and play to the end of the piece.

Andante Grazioso (2nd Mvt. of String Quartet) Op. 74 No. 2 (Haydn, 1793)

DIRECTIONS: The coda sign in measure 4 is used only when playing *the second time through*.
When playing the first time, the coda sign in measure 4 is ignored.

The Suite

A **suite** (SWEET) is a group of excerpts from a larger musical work such as a ballet, opera or musical show. *The original "Nutcracker Suite" consists of eight sections: *Overture, March, Arabian Dance, Chinese Dance, Dance of the Sugar Plum Fairy, Russian Dance, Dance of the Reed Flutes* and *Waltz of the Flowers.* It is probably the most famous suite ever written, and was featured in "Fantasia," the classic animated film by Walt Disney. Five sections from this suite are used on pages 22-25.

A suite may also be a set or group of short instrumental pieces, usually various dance forms, popular during the *baroque* period of music (approximately 1600-1750). Bach and Handel composed music during that time.

The Nutcracker Story

The "Nutcracker" is a full-length ballet in two acts with more than 25 musical pieces. It requires about two hours of performance time. The plot is based on the story *The Nutcracker and The Mouse King,* by E.T.A. Hoffman. The main character is a little girl. At Christmas time she receives many toys and gifts, but her favorite is a wooden nutcracker carved to resemble a toy soldier. She dreams that the nutcracker becomes a handsome prince who rallies the toys to victory in a furious war against the mice. After the battle he escorts her to the *Kingdom of Sweets* where she is entertained by a festival of dances. At the conclusion, all the guests participate in a graceful waltz.

Performing the Suite

It is intended that all five sections of the Nutcracker Suite (pages 22-25) be played as a unit. You probably will want to learn them one or two at a time and eventually put them all together. When playing the suite, there should be a brief pause of a few seconds between each section.

Overture (from "Nutcracker Suite") Op. 71 (Tchaikowsky, 1892)

DIRECTIONS: This piece uses the same eight measure melody two times. The second time it is *transposed* to the key of F major. Many of the fingerings are the same both times. Watch for the staccato notes, short slurs and accents; be sure to play them accurately.

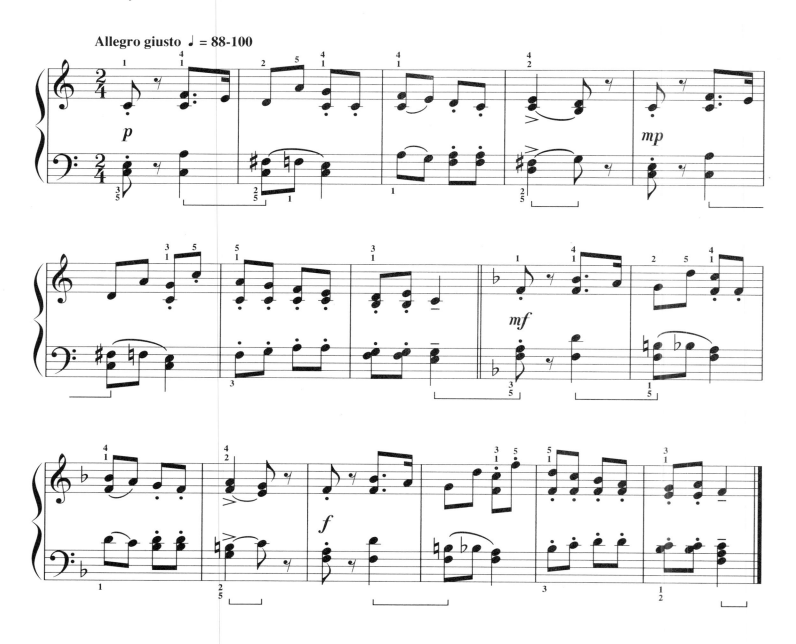

Dotted 8th Rest – Single 16th Note

A dotted 8th rest and a single 16th note appear in the treble staff at the end of the first line of music.
When combined they get one count, the same as a dotted 8th note + 16th note.

March (from "Nutcracker Suite") Op. 71 (Tchaikowsky, 1892)

DIRECTIONS: This piece begins with both hands in the treble clef. Watch for three other clef changes during the music.
   The fingering for the right hand in the last line of music is essential for accurate performance. The critical places are
indicated with a red arrow. Be especially careful to *practice with the correct fingering in the right hand.*

Russian Dance (from "Nutcracker Suite") Op. 71 (Tchaikowsky, 1892)

DIRECTIONS: There are different clef signs on both sides of the double bar line between the 1st and 2nd endings. The treble clef at the end of the *first* ending is a reminder to change the clef when going back to the beginning. The bass clef at the beginning of the *second* ending makes it clear that the treble clef is *not used* there. Neither of these clefs are required; educational editions often have these reminder clefs, but other music may omit them.

Notice the pedal mark at the beginning of the first measure. This is used only during the repeat after the 1st ending.

Dance of the Sugar Plum Fairy (from "Nutcracker Suite") (Tchaikowsky, 1892)

DIRECTIONS: This piece has many accidentals; be sure that you are playing the correct notes. Notice that the third line of music has an *octave higher sign* which affects only the notes in the treble staff. Watch for the *end* of the octave higher sign.

Dance of the Reed Flutes (from "Nutcracker Suite") Op. 71 (Tchaikowsky, 1892)

DIRECTIONS: Watch for the octave higher sign in the 2nd and 3rd measures. The marking **8va**, above the 3rd count in measure 8, means that *only this treble note* is to be played one octave higher.

A new leger line note, D, is used above the treble staff in the 1st ending and also the 2nd ending.

Polyphonic Music

Music usually consists of a melody with some kind of accompaniment. Music may also be composed with two or more melodies sounding simultaneously and blending harmoniously. This kind of music is called **polyphonic** (pah-lih-FAH-nik) meaning literally *many sounds.* When the tunes "Merrily We Roll Along" and "London Bridge" are played simultaneously, they become polyphonic music. Another example of polyphonic music is the well-known Pachelbel's "Canon."

Two Melodies At Once (Example of Polyphonic Music)

DIRECTIONS: This piece is made up of two sections. In the first eight measures, "Merrily We Roll Along" is in the treble staff and "London Bridge" is in the bass staff. In the last eight measures, the positions of the two melodies are exchanged.

As a preparatory, play the treble staff notes alone. Next play the bass staff notes alone. Then play both staffs together, slowly at first, and then gradually increase the tempo. Polyphonic music is good practice for independence of the hands.

It is important to **play both melodies equally loud.** In this piece there is no accompaniment that would normally be subdued. Polyphonic music requires careful listening to be sure each melody can be heard clearly.

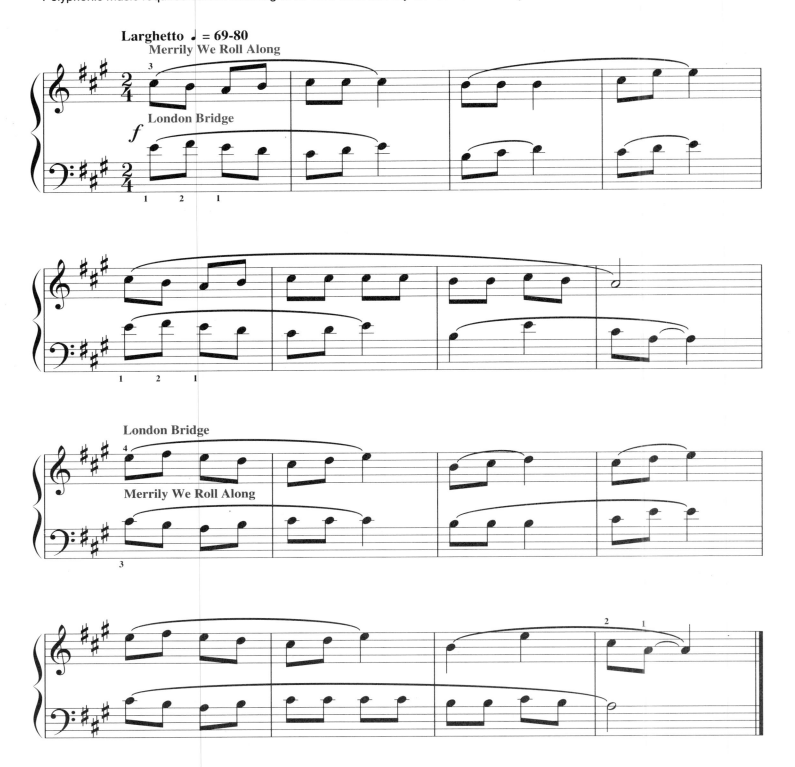

LONDON BRIDGE STORY — "London Bridge," of nursery rhyme fame, has been moved to the United States. After 140 years the venerable London landmark needed repair and was no longer suitable for modern heavy traffic. In the late 1960's it was sold for 2½ million dollars, taken apart (10,276 blocks of granite) and shipped (130,000 tons) to Lake Havasu City, Arizona. It took forty workers twenty-three months to re-assemble it.

The Round

The musical *round* is a form of polyphonic music. In a round, only one melody is used. The piece is formed by repeating the same melody after a lapse of time, usually two or four measures. The overlapping repetitions blend into a harmonious unit.

The pieces on this page are called **2-part rounds** because the same melody is played *two times*. It is also possible to have 3-part and 4-part rounds.

Two Familiar Rounds *(Row, Row, Row Your Boat* and *Frere Jacques)*

DIRECTIONS: As a preparatory, play the treble staff notes alone. Next play the bass staff notes alone. Then play both staffs together, slowly at first, and then gradually increase the speed. Be sure to play both hands **equally loud** throughout.

Watch for *three important changes at the beginning of measure 11:* key signature, time signature and tempo.

Theme from Brandenburg Concerto No. 1, BWV 1046 (4th Movement) (Bach, 1717)

DIRECTIONS: This piece is written in polyphonic style. The bass clef has a melodic part which fits with the treble clef melody. As a preparatory, play the right hand part alone, then the left hand alone before playing both hands together.

The musical form for this piece is **A – B – A¹ – C** (each line of music is one section of the form). The only difference between **A** and **A¹** is that the left hand plays one octave lower during the **A¹** section.

JOHANN SEBASTIAN BACH (BAHKH) 1685-1750 – Germany

Bach is one of the most famous of all composers. A great many of his compositions use polyphonic style. His more complicated works combine four or five simultaneous melodies into one piece of polyphonic music.

Bach wrote an astonishing amount of music during his lifetime – over one-thousand compositions in all. His jobs as composer and music director for various churches and wealthy noblemen required that he provide new music for regular religious services, numerous private concerts and special occasions.

This theme is from the first of six concertos dedicated to the Margrave of Brandenburg. They were written for various combinations of wind and string instruments (violin, viola and cello). The Brandenburg Concerto No. 1 was written for oboe, bassoon, [French] horn, and strings.

3/2 Time Signature

In 3/2 time there are *three counts* per measure. A half note gets one count. The note values are the *same as in cut time* (see page 31). Counting numbers have been printed in red. The **dotted whole note** gets *three* counts (final measure, page 30).

Repeated Note Patterns The bass clef has repeated notes in many measures. These are indicated with red brackets in several measures. Recognizing these repeated notes makes playing the accompaniment much easier.

Turning a Page Without Interrupting the Rhythm

When turning a page of music you should maintain a continuous beat with no interruption or slowing. This is done by not playing some of the notes in one hand, as that hand turns the page. It also involves memorizing the notes for one or two measures before and after the page turn. The page should be turned one or two measures *before the end* — sooner if it is a rapid tempo.

In this piece, turn the page with the right hand during the rests in the last measure of page 29.

I Love Thee, Op. 5 No. 3 (*Grieg, 1863-64)

DIRECTIONS: The metronome speed indicates that a half note gets one beat. At first, you may want to subdivide the counting as shown in measure 1. Then proceed to fewer subdivisions, as in measure 2, or use the counting as shown in measure 3.

Watch for E# (white key sharp) in several places; it is played the same as F (natural). A new note, low A on the 3rd leger line below the bass staff, is found on page 30.

Notice that all of the bass notes in measures 1 – 5 *are the same* as the bass notes in measures 8 –12.

* See page 37 for an explanation and a brief biography of Grieg.

ppp = **Pianississimo** (pee-ah-nih-SISS-ee-moh) means *extremely soft.* It usually requires use of the **soft pedal.**
The soft pedal is *always the farthest to the left* (of 2 or 3 pedals) and is pressed down with the left foot.

Wavy Line = **Rolled Chord** The long *continuous* wavy line extending from the bass staff up through the treble staff (in the final measure) indicates that all notes in both staffs are to be played as **one long continuous rolled chord,** <u>from bottom to top,</u> with bass notes first, followed by treble notes.

If the wavy line is *not continuous* (i.e. if each staff has its own separate wavy line) both chords would be rolled simultaneously.

Hornpipe (Irish Folk Dance)

DIRECTIONS: The counting numbers are shown in red. At first, you may want to practice slowly and subdivide every beat as shown in measure 2. However, as the tempo increases, it becomes awkward to subdivide every count. It is better to think of this piece with just two beats per measure. Try to organize in your mind: in cut time, one count will contain four 8th notes.

Correct fingering is vitally important, especially at this fast tempo.

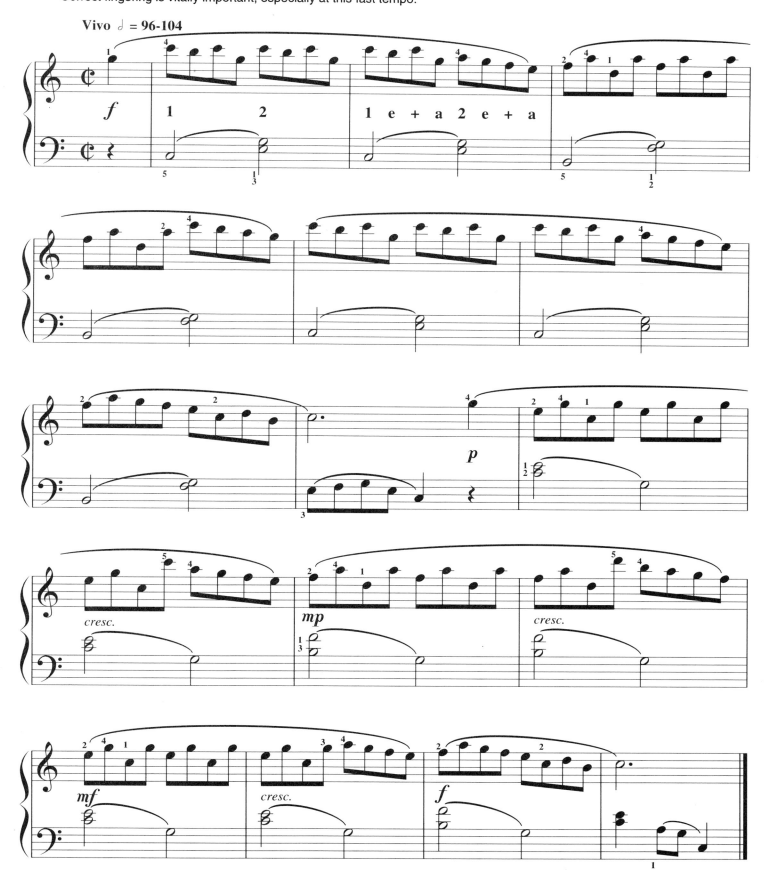

THE FIDDLE — A fiddle is a stringed instrument closely resembling a violin. A fiddle is held under the chin and played with a bow, the same as a violin; however, the style of playing is quite different. A fiddle is used for folk dancing and country music. It is often decorated with inlaid wood, mother-of-pearl or painting. The notes in the treble staff of this piece are common fiddle patterns.

A **hornpipe** is a lively dance done by one person. It was popular among sailors during the 1700's and 1800's.

Gopak (from "Fair of Sorochintsy") (Moussorgsky, 1880)

DIRECTIONS: This piece has many accidentals; watch carefully to be sure you are playing the right notes. At the bottom of page 29, try turning the page with the left hand. If this is too awkward use the right hand instead. You will need to practice the page turn, slowly at first, just as you practice the notes and rhythm.

Allegretto scherzando ♩ = 96-108

*Double Flat

A double flat lowers a note TWO half steps. In this piece, B double-flat is played the same as A. Double flats are used when needed to spell chords with the correct harmony.

MODESTE MOUSSORGSKY (moo-SORG-skee) 1839-1881 – Russia

Moussorgsky is probably best known for his orchestral work "Night On Bald Mountain," featured in Walt Disney's animated film classic "Fantasia." His other well known works are "Pictures At An Exhibition" and the opera "Boris Godunov."

A **gopak** (GO-pak) is a lively Russian folk dance. This music was a ballet sequence in the comic opera "Fair of Sorochintsy."

Review of Treble Leger Lines

Leger line notes above the treble staff are shown here with the letter names in red. Try to remember the note C as a "guidepost" for locating the other notes.

O Wondrous Enchantment, K620 (from "The Magic Flute") (Mozart, 1791)

DIRECTIONS: There are frequent changes of hand position in the treble staff; watch the fingering very carefully. Two new treble clef leger line notes are indicated with red arrows.

WOLFGANG AMADEUS MOZART (MOE-tsart) 1756-1791 – Austria

"The Magic Flute" is one of Mozart's most popular operas. It was written between July and September 1791. Mozart conducted the first performance in Vienna; unfortunately, he died one month later.

"The Magic Flute" is a love story set in Egypt with many complications involving abduction, quest and eventual unification of the lovers. It is a fairy-tale fantasy where good triumphs over evil after trials by ordeal. The "magic flute" is given to the hero, Tamino, to protect him in his search for the captured heroine, Pamina. Papageno, the reluctant ally of Tamino, is aided by magic bells. The music of the flute brings peace and contentment to all those who hear it, even taming wild animals. The bells charm people into dancing. "O Wondrous Enchantment," attesting to these magic instruments, is sung near the end of the first act.

Widespread Accompaniment

In this piece the accompaniment pattern may be too wide to fit comfortably in your hand span. If you are not able to spread your hand wide enough to play all three bass notes legato in each measure, you may lift after the first beat and connect only the notes on the 2nd and 3rd beats, as indicated by the bass clef phrasing. The damper pedal will help to blend the accompaniment notes.

Song of India (from "Sadko") (*Rimsky-Korsakov, 1897)

DIRECTIONS: The white-key flat, C-flat, occurs twice in the treble clef; it is played the same as B natural.
If necessary, refer to page 21 for an explanation of *Coda*.

* See page 37 for an explanation and brief biography of Rimsky-Korsakov.

Review of 9/8 Time

The note values are the same as in 6/8 time. Counting numbers have been printed in red in two sample measures.
If there is a question about the time signature, see page 10.

Les Preludes (Liszt, 1856)

DIRECTIONS: Watch for the change of key in measure 8 and again in measure 17 (page 37).
Be sure to observe the small accent marks that have been added to two of the bass notes in measures 4, 8, 12 and 20.

Page 29: EDVARD GRIEG (GREEG) 1843-1907 – Norway

Grieg is Norway's most famous composer. He was well known as a conductor and concert pianist throughout Europe. His Piano Concerto, written at age 25, and incidental music to "Peer Gynt" are his most famous works. Many of his compositions have a strong nationalistic style, reflecting Norwegian folk music. Grieg was one of the founders of the Norwegian Academy of Music. His wife was a professional singer, and they gave concerts together.

"I Love Thee" is one of a set of four songs collectively titled "The Heart's Melodies," written to lyrics by the Danish author, Hans Christian Anderson. Grieg met Anderson during a stay in Copenhagen. This music is often performed at weddings.

Page 35: NICHOLAS RIMSKY-KORSAKOV (RIM-skee KORE-sah-kov) 1844-1908 – Russia

Rimsky-Korsakov was a prolific composer, writing 17 operas, 4 symphonies, and many pieces of orchestral, choral, vocal, piano and chamber music. His operas were based on fairy tales, legends and Russian folklore.

"Sadko" is a fantasy story of a singer whose voice charms the daughter of the ocean king. It involves a wager with three wealthy merchants, an ocean voyage, a visit to the ocean kingdom and the magical formation of a new river. The "Song of India" is sung by one of the merchants to describe the riches of his country. It is probably Rimsky-Korsakov's best known melody.

Page 36: FRANZ LISZT (LIST) 1811-1886 – Hungary

Liszt is remembered as a flamboyant virtuoso concert pianist, probably the best in the 19th century. He was a brilliant showman and was in great demand in concert halls and in social circles. He composed numerous piano pieces, most of them extremely difficult. He also wrote over 80 pieces of sacred choral music and several hundred pieces of vocal music.

One of Liszt's outstanding contributions as a composer was his development of the "symphonic poem." This is a combination of poetry and literature with music in a form that is a hybrid of an overture and a symphony. He wrote 13 symphonic poems of which "Les Preludes" is the most famous.

Liszt's daughter married Richard Wagner, the famous German opera composer. Liszt conducted and helped to promote many of Wagner's operas.

Page 38: JOHANN SEBASTIAN BACH (BAKH) 1685-1735 – Germany

Bach is one of the best known composers of polyphonic music (see page 26). His most complicated polyphonic music was the **fugue** (FEWG) which combined up to five different themes. He ingeniously mingled these themes in complicated ways. Themes were often transposed, used backwards, upside-down, played faster (with smaller note values) or played slower (with longer note values).

*The year of composition is not known; the letter **c** before the year is an abbreviation of *circa*, meaning *approximately*. Bach scholars disagree as to the origin of this music. Although Bach's authorship cannot be positively confirmed, the piece nonetheless provides an example of his polyphonic style. BWV = Bach-Werke-Verzeichnis, a catalog of Bach's compositions.

Review of Polyphonic Music

This piece is constructed by using two different themes woven together. They are labeled **A** and **B**, with arrows showing where each theme begins.

Both themes are used a second time, starting in the 3rd line of music; however, each theme is transposed five scale degrees higher. The **A** theme is moved to the bass clef; the **B** theme is moved to the treble.

Sonata Theme, BWV 1037 (2nd Mvt.– Sonata for Two Violins) (*Bach, c1720)

DIRECTIONS: Polyphonic music is often harder than it looks. It requires each hand to move independently of the other. Use a much slower tempo at first. You may want to practice each hand separately before putting them together.

Another method of practice is to play the **A** theme alone for the right hand (first two lines of music) followed by the **A** theme alone for the left hand (last two lines of music). The same can be done with the **B** theme.

Polyphonic music is usually played with very little use of the damper pedal; this is done to avoid blurring.

*See bottom of page 37 for an explanation and a brief biography of Bach.

Theme from "Water Music" (Handel, 1717)

DIRECTIONS: This piece has a 3/2 time signature (see page 29). Counting has been printed in red in several measures. Watch for the D.S. al Fine (explained on page 6). Red arrows in the last line of music emphasize where the correct fingering is essential.

GEORGE FREDERICK HANDEL (HAHN-del) 1685-1759 – Germany

Handel is probably best known for the "Hallelujah Chorus" from his oratorio, "Messiah," which is traditionally performed in numerous churches and in concert halls every year – especially during the Easter season.

"Water Music" is an orchestral suite written to honor King George I of England at a festival on the Thames River in London. It was performed by 50 musicians on a barge, which followed the King's boat. The King was so pleased that he asked that the music be repeated three times, even though each performance lasted one hour.

Mattinata (Leoncavallo, 1904)

DIRECTIONS: This piece has many changes of hand position in both hands. Be sure to observe the fingering very carefully. Watch for the *double flat* in the last line of music on page 41. Look up the meaning of *affetuoso* in the dictionary on page 46.

RUGGERO LEONCAVALLO (lay-on-kah-VAL-loh) 1857-1919 – Italy

"Mattinata" is Leoncavallo's best known song, written to his own lyrics as a vocal solo. It is variously known as "'Tis the Day," "Wake With the Dawn," and "Dawn's Greatest Treasure." These translations are not of "Mattinata," but rather of lyrics that occur near the end of the piece.

Leoncavallo is also famous for his opera "Pagliacci," which is in the repertoire of numerous opera companies all over the world. He wrote eight other operas, eight operettas and several dozen songs.

Mexican Hat Dance ("Jarabe Tapatio") (Mexican Folk Song)

DIRECTIONS: This piece has a rapid tempo; notice that the metronome setting is for a *dotted quarter note.* Be sure to observe the correct fingering from the first time you play. The importance of the proper fingering increases as you play at a faster tempo. Look for several repeated patterns in the left hand accompaniment. Each pattern is indicated by a slur.

The Double Sharp

A double sharp (✕) raises a note by *two half steps*. F double-sharp would be played the same as G natural.

Theme from 4th Symphony, Op. 98 (2nd Movement) (Brahms, 1885)

DIRECTIONS: This piece is in the key of E major; there are *four sharps* in the key signature. Be sure to play all F's, C's, G's and D's sharp. Watch for the double-sharps at the end of the last two lines of music.

When returning to the beginning for the D.C. it is assumed you will
1. Resume the original tempo.   2. Make a pedal change on the first beat.

JOHANNES BRAHMS (BRAHMZ) 1833-1897 – Germany

Brahms is one of Germany's greatest composers.   His first piano teacher gave him a thorough knowledge and respect for the music of Bach and Beethoven. An awareness of the high musical standards established by Beethoven's nine symphonies caused Brahms to wait until he had gained Sufficient experience, confidence and maturity as a composer to write his own first symphony (at age 43). Three other symphonies followed within nine years. These four symphonies are still regularly performed by orchestras all over the world.

Brahms established his reputation as a concert pianist and composer by extensive recital tours in Germany, Austria, Hungary, Switzerland and Denmark, often playing his own music. He also was well known as an orchestra conductor.

Clarifying Similar Rhythms

This piece uses three rhythmic patterns which need to be accurate:

1. 8th note triplet.
2. Dotted 8th note and 16th note.
3. Two 8th notes.

The diagram here shows how mathematics can help to clarify the differences between these rhythms. One beat is divided into 12 parts shown by the 12 red lines (12 is the lowest common denominator). The 8th note triplet is printed *above* the red lines. The dotted 8th note and 16th note are printed in the *center*. The two 8th notes are printed *below* in red with a red beam.

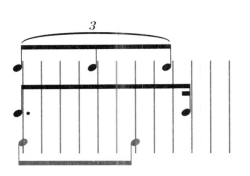

Triumphal March (from "Aida," Act II) (Verdi, 1871)

DIRECTIONS: Watch for the two changes of key on page 45. The first is to A-flat major (all B's, E's, A's and D's are to be played flat). The second key change is back to F major at the end of page 45.

GIUSEPPI VERDI (jee-u-SEHP-ee VAIR-dee) 1813-1901 – Italy

Verdi is one of the most popular of all opera composers. "Aida" (ah-EE-dah) is the most ostentatious of his grand operas requiring large choruses of men's and women's voices, many soloists and a host of non-singing extras including live animals on stage. At its original performance in Cairo, Egypt, there were 300 people in costume on stage at the end of the first act.

Opera houses at the time vied with one another for size and elegance. One of the largest is the Paris Opera. It was elaborately decorated like a palace with a huge lobby, grand staircases, crystal chandeliers, beautiful stonework and fancy molded plaster. Numerous works of art such as paintings and sculptures were displayed. Modern opera audiences continue the "dress-up" tradition that comes from these opulent theatres.

You are now ready to progress to Schaum's **MAKING MUSIC at the PIANO, Level 5**.

MUSIC DICTIONARY

Terms not listed here may be found in the INDEX (page 48) or on the REFERENCE PAGES (Front and Rear Inside Covers).

Most musical terms are Italian, because music writing began in Italy. The accented syllable is shown in *capital letters.*

See the Front and Rear Reference Pages for illustrations of basic music elements and correlation of notes with their keyboard location.

Terms listed here are limited to those commonly found in Level Four methods and supplements. For a more complete listing get the Schaum **DICTIONARY OF MUSICAL TERMS** With over 1550 words in 96 pages, it contains most terms found in program notes for recordings, concerts and newspaper reviews, including frequently used Italian, French, and German words. It is helpful in working with band and orchestra instruments, vocalists and choral groups.

---

accelerando (ahk-sell-er-ON-doh) Becoming gradually faster in tempo.

adagio (ah-DAH-jee-oh) Slow, slowly.

affetuoso (ah-fet-too-OH-soh) Affectionately.

agitato (ahd-jih-TAH-toh) Agitated, restless.

alla marcia (ah-lah MAHR-chee-ah) March style.

allargando (ah-lahr-GAHN-doh) Gradually slower and louder.

allegretto (ah-leh-GRET-toh) A little slower than *allegro.*

allegro (ah-LEG-grow) Fast, quickly.

andante (ahn-DAHN-tay) Moderately slow; at a comfortable walking pace.

andantino (ahn-dahn-TEE-noh) A little faster than *andante.*

anima (AH-nee-mah) Spirit, life, animation.

animato (ah-nee-MAH-toh) Lively, spirited.

a tempo (ah TEHM-poh) Return to the previous tempo.

basso marcato (BAH-so mahr-CAH-toh) Emphasize the bass notes.

bravura (brah-VOO-rah) Boldness, brilliance.

brillante (bree-LAHN-teh) Brilliant, showy.

brio (BREE-oh) Vigor, spirit, gusto.

cantabile (cahn-TAH-bil-lay) Singing style.

cantando (cahn-TAHN-doh) Singing style.

chamber music Music involving a small group of performers for a small hall or parlor. Usually for various instrumental combinations from two to ten players.

coda (KOH-dah) Extra musical section added at the end of a piece of music to emphasize the conclusion.

common time 4/4 meter. Time signature is: ¢

con (KONE) With.

concerto (kon-SHARE-toh) Long composition for solo instrument accompanied by band or orchestra displaying the talents of the solo performer.

cresc. = crescendo (cre-SHEN-doh) Gradually increasing in loudness. Also abbreviated with the sign: ◁

D.C. al coda = da capo al coda (dah KAH-poh ahl KODE-ah) Return to the beginning and repeat up to the coda sign (⊕). Then skip to the coda and play to the end. See page 21.

D.C. al fine = da capo al fine (dah KAH-poh ahl FEE-nay) Return to the beginning and repeat, ending at the word *fine.*

decr. = decrescendo (deh-creh-SHEN-doh) Gradual decrease in loudness.

delicato (dell-ih-CAH-toh) Delicately.

dim. = diminuendo (di-min-you-END-oh) Becoming gradually less loud. Also abbreviated with the sign: ▷

dissonance (DISS-uh-nunce) Combination of simultaneous musical sounds that are unpleasant or harsh to the listener. See page 16.

dolce (DOL-chay) Sweetly, softly.

doloroso (doh-loh-ROH-soh) Sadly, sorrowfully.

drammatico (dreh-MAH-tee-koh) Dramatically.

D.S. al coda = dal segno al coda (dahl SEN yo ahl KOH-dah) Return to the sign (𝄋) and repeat up to the coda sign (⊕). Then skip to the coda and play to the end. See page 35.

D.S. al fine = dal segno al fine (dahl SEN yo ahl FEE-nay) Return to the sign and repeat, ending at the word *fine.*

dynamic marks Symbols and words indicating changes of loudness.

eleganza (el-leh-GAHN-zah) Elegance, grace.

energico (eh-NAIR-jee-koh) Energetic, powerful.

enharmonic Writing the same musical pitch in two different ways, such as C# and D-flat.

espressivo (ehs-preh-SEE-voh) With expression and emotion.

etude (ay-TOOD) Music study-piece to develop technical skills.

expression marks Musical terms and instructions affecting tempo, loudness and mood.

8va [When placed above] play one octave *higher* than written.

8va [When placed below] play one octave *lower* than written.

fff = fortississimo (fohr-tih-SISS-ee-moh) Extremely loud.

fine (FEE-nay) End.

fz = forzando (fohr-TSAHN-doh) With force, energy, strongly accented.

giocoso (jee-oh-KOH-soh) Humorously, playfully.

grandioso (grahn-dee-OH-soh) Dignified, majestic.

grazioso (gra-tsee-OH-soh) Gracefully.

giusto (JOOS toh) With precise, steady tempo.

larghetto (lahr-GET-oh) A little faster than *largo.*

largo (LAHR-goh) Very slow, solemn.

legato (lah-GAH-toh) Notes played in a smooth, connected manner with no interruption in sound.

leggiero (led-jee-AIR-oh) Light, delicate.

lento (LEN-toh) Slow, but not as slow as *largo*.

L.H. = Left Hand

maestoso (my-ess-TOH-soh) Majestic, dignified.

marcato (mahr-CAH-toh) Marked, emphasized.

melodia marcato (meh-LOH-dee-ah mahr-CAH-toh) Emphasize the melody notes, usually in the treble.

meno (MAY-noh) Less.

metronome (MET-roh-nome) Device to determine tempo or speed in music, measured in beats per minute. See page 15.

misterioso (miss-teer-ee-OH-soh) Mysteriously.

M.M. = Maelzel's metronome. See *metronome*.

moderato (mah-dur-AH-toh) Moderately.

molto (MOHL-toh) Very, much.

mosso (MOHS-soh) Moving, animated.

non troppo (NOHN TROHP-poh) Not too much.

octave (AHK-tiv) Interval of an 8th; the top and bottom notes have the same letter name.

op. = **opus** (OH-puss) Unit of musical work usually numbered in chronological order. May be a composition of any length from a short single piece, a collection of pieces, to a full symphony or opera.

passione (pah-see-OH-neh) Passion, emotion.

pesante (peh-SAHN-teh) Heavy, weighty.

phrase (FRAZE) Group of successive notes dividing a melody or accompaniment pattern into a logical section. This is comparable to the way sentences divide a text into sections. See page 17.

piu (PEE-oo) More.

poco (POH-koh) Little.

poco a poco (POH-koh ah POH-koh) Little by little, gradually.

ppp = **pianississimo** (pee-ah-nih-SISS-ee-moh) Extremely soft.

presto (PRESS-toh) Very fast, faster than *allegro*.

primo (PREE-moh) 1) First. 2) First part or player. In a piano duet the first (upper) part is labeled *primo,* the second (lower) part is labeled *secondo*.

rall. = **rallentando** (rah-lenn-TAHN-doh) Gradually growing slower.

R.H. = Right Hand

rit. = **ritardando** (ree-tahr-DAHN-doh) Gradually decreasing the rate of tempo.

rubato (roo-BAH-toh) Small slowings and accelerations of the tempo of a piece at the discretion of the performer or conductor.

scherzando (skare-TSAHN-doh) Playfully, jokingly, humorously.

secondo (seh-KAHN-doh) Second part or player. See *primo*.

semplice (SEMM-plee-chay) Simple, plain.

sempre (SEMM-pray) Always, constantly.

sf = **sfz** = **sforzando** (sfor-TSAHN-doh) Sudden emphasis or accent on a note or chord.

sostenuto (soss-teh-NOO-toh) Sustained; holding notes to full value.

spiritoso (spir-ih-TOH-soh) Animated, with spirit.

symphony (SYM-foh-nee) Large piece of music written for orchestra.

tempo di marcia (TEMM-poh dih MAHR-chee-ah) March tempo.

tempo di valse (TEMM-poh dih VALSE) Waltz tempo.

tempo I Return to the original tempo.

ten. = **tenuto** (teh-NOO-toh) Sustained, held to full value.

tonic First degree of a major or minor scale.

tranquillo (trahn-KWILL-oh) Tranquil, quiet.

vivace (vee-VAH-chay) Lively, quick.

vivo (VEE-voh) Lively, animated.

Suggested SHEET MUSIC SOLOS

• = Original Form   ✓ = Chord Symbols   (All Published or Distributed by Schaum Publications, Inc.)

48

KEY SIGNATURES: MAJOR and RELATIVE MINOR
(See Pages 18 and 19 for Information on Harmonic Minor Scales)

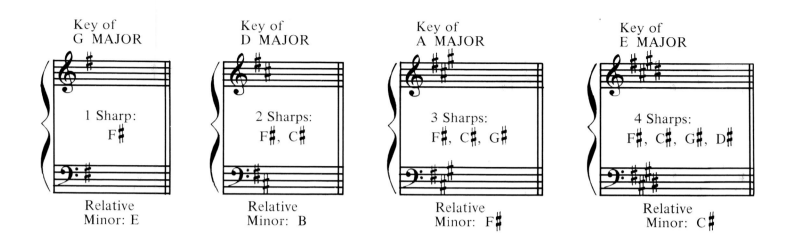

Key of
G MAJOR
1 Sharp:
F#
Relative Minor: E

Key of
D MAJOR
2 Sharps:
F#, C#
Relative Minor: B

Key of
A MAJOR
3 Sharps:
F#, C#, G#
Relative Minor: F#

Key of
E MAJOR
4 Sharps:
F#, C#, G#, D#
Relative Minor: C#

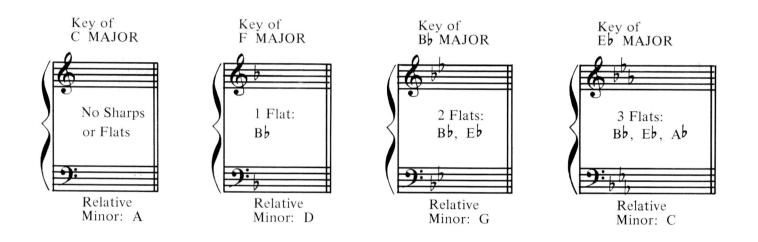

Key of
C MAJOR
No Sharps or Flats
Relative Minor: A

Key of
F MAJOR
1 Flat:
Bb
Relative Minor: D

Key of
Bb MAJOR
2 Flats:
Bb, Eb
Relative Minor: G

Key of
Eb MAJOR
3 Flats:
Bb, Eb, Ab
Relative Minor: C

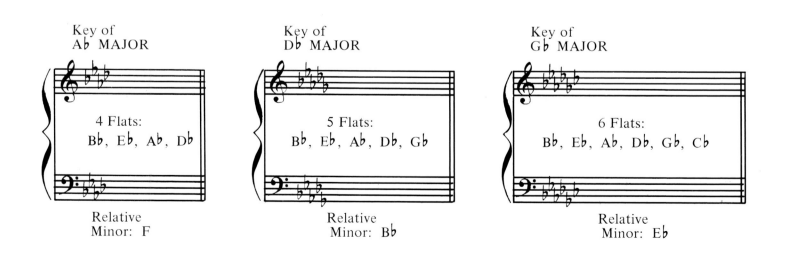

Key of
Ab MAJOR
4 Flats:
Bb, Eb, Ab, Db
Relative Minor: F

Key of
Db MAJOR
5 Flats:
Bb, Eb, Ab, Db, Gb
Relative Minor: Bb

Key of
Gb MAJOR
6 Flats:
Bb, Eb, Ab, Db, Gb, Cb
Relative Minor: Eb

Also See **Reference Page** (Front Inside Cover) and **Music Dictionary** (page 46)

SCHAUM · · · VARIETY FOR ALL LEVELS